Musings on My World

Musings on My World

Carol Gabica

TAVA Mountain Publishing

TAVA Mountain Publishing
Melbourne, FL

Paperback ISBN: 978-1-953667-03-8

Library of Congress Control Number: 2021923010

First paperback edition: December 2021

Cover art by Becky Fox (innervsion@gmail.com)
Book layout and design by TAVA Mountain Publishing

Dedication

To that wonderful band of women who convinced me to do this undertaking and gave me the motivation to move forward. I will forever be in your debt when you spurred me on during the terrible numbing of the pandemic years of 2020 and 2021, when the whole world was in pain. You know your names; you know my love.

To my friends at Center for Spiritual Living Space Coast who let me exercise my voice and pushed me to contribute more, thank you so much for being my champions.

To Mrs. Freeman, my English teacher at Middleton High School, Middleton, Idaho, who somehow convinced this secretly shy girl that she could write.

To my beloved family who always stood at my back, holding me up when I felt my knees collapse.

My humble thanks, I hope this book does not betray your confidence in me,

This is for you all.

Acknowledgement

What a trio we make!

Barbara Loftus: author, entrepreneur, engineer, program manager—my editor and publisher.

Becky Fox: beautifully gentle – yet strong as steel, a gifted artist whose works grace this volume.

Thanks to you both for making this a reality!

Table of Contents

About the Author

Abundance

I remember as a little girl

The yellow magazine with pictures —

Pictures from all over the world.

My Mom paid for it by saving money from her house allowance.

We turned the pages together and saw visions of the vast world —

Huts and igloos, caves and mansions,

Smiling women showing their mouths empty of teeth

Stirring a pot over an open fire

Showing off their three goats.

All over the world, faces alighted with smiles

Celebrating the ability to share their pride, their happiness,

Holding each other together, sharing what counts

Abundance of love—in war, in peace, in pestilence

Abundance of spirit between the yellow magazine covers

As I open the yellow cover of my life,

I thank God for

The ping of a text from a friend

The squirrels entertaining my cat

The neighbor bringing in my garbage can

The flowers shaking off the winter cold

I see the title of my story under the yellow cover

Abundance

Fly Little Girl, Fly

The cool breeze was perfect for an outdoor dinner. Small restaurants and cozy hotels surrounded the park, and the tinkle of laughter could be heard bouncing from corner to corner of the guarded compound.

As I contemplated ordering monkey for the first time, the sky suddenly lit with the thunderous sound of an explosion, mere blocks away. Silence filled the square as all eyes moved toward the scene of the explosion. Moments passed before the sound of conversation broken with laughter filled the compound space again . . .***Dinner in Bogota.***

The car sped across the countryside. The driver silently concentrated on the road ahead. His classic features were augmented by a body obviously trained with military precision.

The mountains in the background were beautifully outlined as the sun rose over the valley. 80 mph —85 as we entered the no man's land and reality replaced my reverie. Clusters of what once were villages, houses with only one remaining wall, churches, and mosques defaced—crumbling.

As we moved further from the Serbian border, new houses started to spring up. Children began to appear, and groups of people talking. Workers were everywhere—building, building. Hope, life, excitement, victory over genocide! . . . ***Pristina.***

The master design of the cobbled street passed under my feet—world renown pattern of black and white. Music followed the beach for miles, and the colored lights sparkled off the white surf.

As I walked back to my hotel, I was caught up in the magic that floated on the warm breeze. Movement in the courtyard I passed drew my concentration away from the colorful waves. As my eyes adjusted to the shadows, I saw benches surrounding a courtyard. Packed together, huddling under each bench—children. 20-30 in this small park—some merely toddlers—girls, all of them girls! Girls are valued among the desperately poor only as prostitutes—boys can work. So, the parents send the girls away to survive on their own . . . *Rio.*

Four floors—no elevator! I'm reminded of what lousy shape I am in—oxygen! Please! The doors were simple—nothing ornate. Cameras flashed as the ambassador and I were greeted by the president. His English was hesitant but better than he thought it to be. Statehood—the next new country in the world—dedication and determination . . . *Kosovo.*

I rounded the corner in the FAA Command Center and saw the plaque. It's small and uneventful, but its message is memorable. 4576 specs on the national screen—average busy moment CONUS traffic—slowly, painstakingly going to black—representing safe landings—representing no take offs. Controllers—stoic, fearless, multi-tasking life-savers—cried . . . *9/11.*

The airport was small, packed with passengers awaiting flights-and cold. The big brown eyes of the girl watched me—the foreigner—as I sat surrounded by my luggage. She flipped over my luggage tag—I flipped it back and she giggled—her eyes sparkled. She silently crawled up on the chair beside me and cuddled into the crook of my arm—snuggled into my fur coat. As she slept, her parents smiled at me—we couldn't speak to each other—we didn't have to . . . **Winter in Slovenia**.

The transfer ticket line was long, but I had quite a lay-over. Fatigues and back-packs, short-cropped hair—on their way to Iraq. I bought a lot of beer that day while we exchanged stories of home . . . **Amsterdam.**

He had broken his glasses the day before, so tape held them together as we drove toward the customer location. His shave showed a few missed places, and he wore a narrow tie—he hates ties. When we entered the room of Italian suits and stony eyes, credibility seemed miles away. The gauntlet was tossed, and my broken-glassed security specialist responded for five hours—no one left the room . . . **Geek 1— Italian Suits 0.**

5AM—not yet light—what is that sound! Dogs began barking—waves of birds flying—call to prayer—my alarm clock . . . **Somewhere.**

The sound! Like a semi-truck revving its engine at the side of our bed—unbelievable roar. The eye stalled offshore and the 145 mph winds beat us for hours trying to find a breech that would allow it to steal our roof. Silence—the eye! Standing on a step ladder to see over the shutters, I saw the yellow-green sky—round two coming . . . ***Hurricane Francis.***

The rental car seems to know its way—I'm glad because the old landmarks are disappearing. As I turn the corner, I see the beautiful yard. Flowers, trees—beautifully cared for. My role model, my idol, the wind beneath my wings—the person who knows me the most—the place to rest . . . ***Mother.***

The plane was late—as usual. Finally in my own bed—the rhythmic breathing of my husband—our cat nestled between us, purring—my mind slowly stopping its whirling. How blessed, this little girl from Middleton . . . ***Home.***

Ourselves

Lightning fills the skies; rain plummets the roof and screens,

Sending torrents of wake-up calls

I am here, I am here, I am here

Reminding us perhaps, through sound and light

I am here, I am here

A wake-up call to perhaps remind us that

WE are not in charge of the universe, but in charge of how we interact with it

WE participate in this great interaction between flesh and spirit

Our choice—our choice

We can not calm the thunderous sounds of nature

We can celebrate them

We can embrace how it fills our essence as a great reminder

Let thunder roll—let the lightning remind us

We are in charge of how we expose ourselves

If we chose to let it be an extension of the Spirit within us

Then we truly bless those around us.

Old Friends

Two books share a shelf on my bookcase, gathering today's dust as they share with me— yesterday.

One's leather cover is cracked and ragged, being held together by a necktie almost disintegrated by time, carried in the trenches of WW1, a lock of my grandmother's hair still tucked inside like a warm embrace.

Now tightly protecting its bounty is a handkerchief embroidered by her—locking away the treasures that lie within—"One God, Do unto others, For God so loved the world"— passed from generation to generation—ancient words captured in a book over 100 years old—shared by family, clutched in moments of joy and sorrow as if the words were new—or maybe a renewal.

The second book took a different path to my shelf. It came from Tel Aviv and opened from the back. One side Hebrew, one side English, passing its message on through generations—"One God, who forsaketh not those who seek thee."

Both friends, handed through the generations, symbols of man's effort to express the essence of God.

But they do not stop on my bookshelf—they will travel further—they will touch the hands of my granddaughter and with love be shared with those who come after. For their story never dies because they are:

Old Friends.

Spiritual Document

Half way through what I dreaded—a book as boring as a college text—a workbook and assignments

A class full of people who were already engaged in a thought process that I didn't understand

Feeling limited, feeling stupid, feeling lost

Used to being a major contributor, thought leader, someone of distinction—but all of that is gone and my ego is sucking for air, a lost limb

Rev would see my frustration and put in words I could understand, embrace, feel in touch with

Nights became, rather than rehashing my failures, even focused on giving praise

"Thank you, God, for healing me and relieving my pain"

My Mantra, My hope

Then more frustration, not understanding, not internalizing, not worthy

My self-hate raised its head, so I had to look at it—again and again and again

So many screaming ghosts, fat, ugly, limited, not strong enough, don't exercise, not in control, drink too much, don't care, want to die before I am totally handicapped—bla, bla, the voices resounding

Over and over in my head—not worthy, not loved, not, not, not—and alone, so very alone

10

Pity me, Pity myself, I want Michael back, I want Momma
back, the only people who truly loved ME

Not the mask I wear, not the comic, the cheerleader, but the
insecure me

I can't "intellectualize" my feelings, my hope, my dreams

Can't stand the pontification of intellectual views for what is
to me a very emotional rebirth

Want to run and hide but I won't because I still find peace in
the words

I will keep seeking my inner peace—wherever that leads me

Then I read Albert Einstein—of ALL people—super
brilliant, one who deserves above all others to pontificate

"Strange is our situation here upon the earth. Each of us
comes for a short visit, not knowing why, yet sometimes
seeming to divine purpose. From the standpoint of daily life,
however, there is one thing we do know: That we are here
for the sake of others . . . for the countless unknown souls
with whose fate we are connected by a bond of sympathy.
Many times a day, I realize how much my outer life is built
upon the labors of people, both living and dead, and how
earnestly I must exert myself in order to give in return as
much as I have received."

Humor in the Force

What good is life if you can't laugh?

That intake of breath and rapid exhaling

Sometimes so hard you cry a bit

Relieving the self-imposed stress that surrounds us daily unless we

Breathe, hopefully with an attached laugh

That special time when we really experience "the force that is with us"

That "force" that has our back

Gives us the ability to experience true joy

Ability to laugh out loud in a public setting

When blessed by the company of a friend who understands our child within

Peeking out to pull a prank or say something inappropriate

Laugh out loud

Because the Force is with us

And the Force loves humor

Just watch the squirrels chasing each other from tree to tree in absolute hilarious antics

Watch people racing their cars from lane to lane to reach the same stop light

Not understanding that there is humor there if you care to see it

We are surrounded by whatever "Force" we choose to honor

But I am blessed, as you, with a Force that allows us to laugh as well as cry

May the Force be with you.

Desertion

Time to STOP the Memories!
I was a stupid, naive, star-struck beginner in the life of
woman-hood
You were handsome and dashing in your uniform
Always knew how to make me swoon
Told me your life with your wife was over
Introduced me to your beautiful daughters
They were looking forward to me "being their teacher"
When they moved to join you
You just disappeared
Just shut down
Just walked out
Of course, you thought, I should have understood
It was a fling
How dare I think it was real
How silly could I be
You crushed me for years
For years I dated people I knew would leave me
They always did because I chose correctly
My pain was tangible
Then the trail of desertion ended
My escape was unexpected
I found someone who loved me back.

Michael

Thank You, God

The desk clock continues its ticking, repetitiously counting the seconds of the minutes of the hours of the days

Reminding me that I am here

Reminding me that there is more to the steady beat than the time between meetings

The cat's tail brushes the backside of my legs as she paths her way under my desk

Finding a place to curl up on my toes

Adding to the steady beat with her melodious purr

My walls are filled with pictures of love—some old, some new

Tick, Tick, Tick—faces frozen in time but not in heart

As I breathe to the rhythm of life—my life

Lest I forget how blessed I am, I whisper my favorite prayer

Thank you, God.

Partners

An extremely poignant word, especially this weekend

Dads and their off-spring facing off the world together—
partners

Celebration of the emancipation proclamation's final hold-
out in Galveston—celebration of partnership between the
oppressed and those who really want the barriers to fall—
partners

That special person who holds our heart and our hand as we
face the day—partners

Tiny birds driving off the crow who is trying to attack their
nest—partners

The crazed woman who screams at the two hawks who try to
attack the bunny in her yard—bunny survives—woman and
bunny celebrate another day—unlikely but significant
partners

Partners—Watching out for the other

Lending a helping hand

Bound together, sometimes inexplicably, but bound

Spirit within that binds all things as one

Allows us to be a partner in the universe

The glue that makes us whole, makes us count, gives us
reason

Spirit as our partner

As it should be, as it is.

I'd Never Leave You

As I look at your smiling face in the photo above my desk,
so very you

The memories explode

And I still get that feeling to my bones

I can still feel the touch of your hand on my neck

Just unbelievable peace

Throughout my body and soul

Nothing will ever replace that touch

Nor the loneliness that lack provides

I ache for that touch every day

Deeply ache

For your hand on my shoulder

Knowing I am not alone.

A Circle of Women

In the darkness of my day
I watch my windows weep
Then, touching my cheek,
Discover the tears are mine.

Began and ended with the purr of my cat—bringing me back
to life after the death of my heart, my soul, my spirit—my
reason to open my eyes again

My dear Michael

But Tu needed food and pets and love and attention—and
she, of all of us, missed him the most and probably most
profoundly—realized rather than rationalized death.

So with her the circle began—with her needing me to
survive. My recognition of the circle began—slowly, very
slowly as I clawed my way through the slime of loneliness,
desolate and unfathomable desperation, pulled back into life
by a circle of women—begun by my cat and ranks closing
around me by my life-giving friends and mother—breathing
the air for me so that I would survive

A circle of women.

He's Gone

I stood in front of the mirror
Putting on my mask of courage
Foundation, eyeliner and mascara
Adding a touch of blush to lighten up my white face
Heading for my car—I literally forgot where I was going
Then the blur of which street to take
Cars were whirling by me
A pickup sped by me at the intersection
Waving a one finger salute as he cut in front of me and
hurried to his destination
It seemed that I was in everyone's way
Forgetting my turn and having to retrace my path
To the blare of horns and snarling faces
Numb and lost, I was interfering in the lives of others
My car took up two parking spaces
I didn't seem to be able to make it go between the lines
A glare from a woman behind me as I fled the car
Elevator chattering as people headed to their desks
I watched the numbers pass overhead
Noise in my ears as someone tried to get by me
The papers placed in front of me
 A copy of the death certificate in my sweating hand
Sign and be done then I will be safe to flee
Back to my cocoon, my walls of protection closed around
me
He's gone
He's gone.
Emptiness.

Michael

I wonder if "happy transition" is appropriate for you—It isn't for me, but I guess this isn't about me but about you.

I really hope there is a place where you are laughing with your Mom and have introduced her to mine—I never really thought about it until today, but I bet they would like each other.

I know you and Unk and Harry are having a ball together—I look to the sky periodically and know you are fly fishing up there. I don't know why I see you as this, but it is the best vision I can bless you with.

I remember all the time your struggle to survive. You were not going to leave us. My biggest regret is that I believed the aide when she said, don't touch him—I really wanted to hold you—I still want to hold you—I was there my dear, so was Nathan—we were by your side—praying, hoping for you to go swiftly without pain but you just refused to leave this plane—you struggled to stay with us, maybe to stay with me—I was numb and in breathless pain. Once you left it was just, and still is, numb, ignore, avoid—I have failed you—I am fat and drink and feeling sorry for myself daily—you would be kicking my ass—I wish you were.

Now we are in the midst of a pandemic—not sure that that is not necessary—a balance in our world in which we are so divided, so angry, so afraid. If you were here to hear Trump, I think you would be coming off the couch with a lock of your hair in my hand as I rubbed your head—damn I miss that—bet you figure you would never hear that huh?

I miss your touch, your hugs, your standing as tall as you could so I couldn't kiss you and us laughing, your quiet wisdom, the way men gravitated to you—even my today management. I think—your stories, your arm across my back, just your touch—oh my God your touch I miss it the most—it never stopped filling my cracks which now are so wide open and so painful. I long for your touch, Momma's hugs—but your touch my dear Michael—feeling safe, feeling safe, feeling loved.

Beloved Mom

What Do You Give?

What do you give someone who IS everything?
A trinket, a charm—someone else's verse?

What do you give someone who IS everything?
Your heart, your soul?

How does it measure against motherhood?
So weak, so hopeless in comparison

On this day of celebration
That has turned into packages galore

Maybe what I give is a reflection—
A mirror reflection of my mother

What better gift than your own reflection
Through the eyes of someone who loves you.

Mom

I still have many days a week that 7 PM reminds me to call my Mom:

208-585-2947.

My fingers are still trained to touch those keys, knowing my mother was on the other end.

Every night, no matter what strange country I might be in—time to call Mom—time to touch base.

Time to feel unquestioning love—time to be at peace—time to let my shields down—time to call Mom.

I come from a little town in the Boise, Idaho valley called Middleton. My school system included all of the farming country around, and my class still averaged 36. If there was anyone in the entire school or church or community that did not know, or know of, my Mom—it was their loss. She was Middleton's Mom. Self-made supporter of youth, she made us all feel like we had everything the big towns had.

She learned to decorate cakes like the wedding cake providers and brought her cupcakes to the classroom as a Room Mother—decorated with iced roses—the teachers would have to do a drawing to see who would get "Della's cupcakes" while the rest were stuck with plain old cupcakes.

Halloween meant trick-or-treaters getting big pumpkin-faced cookies, hand made and given to every kid at the door—we were their favorite place to land till the kids from the neighboring towns heard about it and she had to turn out the light at 7PM.

Special was her livelihood—it kept her sane in a town too small for her but gave her a reason to share her love. She taught us to give, taught us to love—it wasn't till much later that we discovered that we truly didn't have any money. She magically made the dollars stretch to allow her to sew our clothes, do amazing gift wrap, feed lunch to children we brought home unannounced to her because they "forgot" their lunch.

I remember how she taught us to pay bills. She had a notebook where she recorded every bill and paperclipped them to the top of the page. When she ran out of money for that month she would pay the bill she missed the month before and move another bill to the paperclip for the next month, thus making the money stretch without upsetting the companies—knowing Dad would not give her any more.

She was indeed Middleton's mother: Room Mother, MYF mother, driving the back country roads to pick up kids that couldn't attend without a ride—always there. Riding the school buses to take us to the zoo, the roller skate rink— which was such a special treat, and one my knees and I remember still!

And as we grew into our teens, she brought a dance instructor in from the big town of Caldwell to teach us how to dance. We even went on TV! And of course, Mom drove us and helped make our costumes.

Middleton's Mom.

When my sister was in an auto accident, she spent every day by her side. She saw me limping and found out that I was wearing a pair of Betty's shoes because the soles of mine had worn out. Mom took the time to notice and took me out of school the next morning to go get me shoes before going back to be with Betty. She had X-ray vision—straight to your heart, never missing a beat, even when she had to be so tired she couldn't breathe.

Middleton's Mom—Our Mom.

She was there for me when I left college for a semester and joined my hippie friends in Idaho Falls. It had to have cut her in half, but you could never tell it. I remember when my friend and I got a ride from one of her friends from California—hair past his shoulders, hippie van intact. We drove from Moscow, Idaho to Idaho Falls and stopped to stay overnight in—yes—Middleton, Idaho. Mom welcomed my friends with pallets on the living room floor while Dad watched TV in the family room. That morning I went to the kitchen, and there was Mom. She stood at the kitchen window on a Sunday morning with a California hippie van sitting in our driveway and watched the Mormon church attendees gawk so hard one of the ladies walked off the sidewalk, and my Mom howled with laughter.

I could go on, but you get the drift. My mother, my stalwart, my friend—she kept me going when I was so very afraid: 208-585-2947 Mom.

When my beloved Michael knew he was dying, I had a business trip to Boise, which meant I got to go see Mom. He told me he wanted to go too—as a surprise—which was a rarity. So I drove into Mom's carport and saw her waiting at the window. I will never forget the look on her face when she saw Michael with me.

I went to my meeting, and Michael spent the day with Mom. Though I asked, neither would ever tell me what they discussed. I only know that Mom held on, despite the odds, for an entire year after I lost my beloved Michael. Giving me a reason to make a call—every night at 7 PM—a reason to go on.

I will always believe it was a deal made by the two most powerful contributors to my life:

208-585-2947.

Good Deeds

Good Deeds

Have you ever noticed they never come with an instruction book?

Insert battery A in slot B—tighten notch C

Money back guarantee

Not with Good Deeds—they happen when your eyes really see—and your heart opens

Most times you don't really know you exercised your caring muscle

It just had to happen—that good deed

Not expecting even a nod—not thinking one is necessitated

Just following your heart

Letting it open doors for you

Letting you notice those things that others miss

Filling that undefinable gap in the life of others

Good Deed? Or just celebrating life shared

Holding the needs, dreams and wishes of others

In the same esteem you hold your own

Good Deeds? Are there really such things?

Or is it truly just living with an open heart

Guided by God, guided by caring

Holding a hand, hugging a shoulder, lifting a burden, carrying a weight too heavy but unseen

Good deeds—sharing the journey we call life.

Little Brown Purse

My Mom had a little brown coin purse

It was the one she would hand me when she sent me to the grocery store

It's real leather and has aged with me as it aged with her

It is the one thing I brought home when we sent her off

I carry it with me all the time

And today I fixed an area where the stitching was split, and a gap of light shown through to the inside

Little brown purse

Swells my insides when I touch it

Reminds me of those hands that held it

She never seemed to know that I put money into it whenever I went to the store

Little brown purse

We all own one you know

That sacred place that we hold to our heart

The thing that lets all the love build and peace surround us for just a second

Might be a something or a someone, might be a scene out the window or one inside

But we all own a little brown purse

It's good to hold it tightly because the Spirit lives in it, lives in the memories and the feelings it arouses

Fills the blank holes that nothing else can fill

Little brown purse

Hold it close and say with me, "Thank you, God."

Montana Loves

Beloved Sheila

Many short years ago my husband gave me a gift

The greatest gift I have ever received

Not wrapped up with gilded bows or sparkles shining in the
light

Looking back, I know it was with some trepidation

Would something so very special be special to all

I still remember the clamp of my stomach and sweat on my
brow

So afraid the gift would reject the receiver, so afraid

A world I had never entered, did not understand

My high heels sunk into the driveway

And my new world began

The greatest gift I have ever received

My Michael gave me you.

Let Freedom Ring

The 4th of July

A special touch point for all of us

Let Freedom Ring

Makes me remember and project

My past memories of picnics and celebration

Of driving to Montana with a carload of fireworks for the grandchildren—and the adult child in all of us

Of BBQ's and back yard fires, marshmallows and late-night storytelling

Grandchildren cuddled up in my chair as the fire turned to embers

The touch of my husband's hand

The sense of love and peace

The sense of belonging to a greater circle that encompassed our country, our world

Let freedom ring

Today I breathe in the peace that goes beyond the 4th

The peace that comes only from the spirit within

And whisper a quiet prayer

Let freedom ring.

Great Grandson

He's 2 ½ going on 20

My great grandson—what a spark

Facetime is always a joy

I can never tell what will happen

His mom just shakes her head and turns away to laugh

His latest toy is Dad's flashlight

He showed me how to turn it on

Taking it to the closet he shows me

It lights up the corners

"What are you looking for?"

See g'ma see?

See, See?

Yes, I see

I feel

I know

I look in his face, his mother's face, and yes—even mine

And I see God.

9/11

9/11

Note: I moved to Melbourne, FL, on 9/14/2001. I was on the first flight out after 9/11 from Seattle for my new job. My husband was in Russia, fly-fishing on an environmental impact study of Chernobyl on the fisheries in Russia.

My first day on the Melbourne beach outside my hotel:

It rained so hard I hid

Under the steps to the sea.

The thunder echoed in my ears

As rain pelted down on me—seemingly from all directions.

I heard myself shouting out,

"Why God, Why?"

Tears ran faster than the pelting rain.

Why?

In my heart the voice repeated

Forgive.

Forgive.

But I can't forgive, I can't

And the voice replied, I CAN

Learn from me.

The Day Controllers Cried

There is nothing quite like watching Air Traffic Controllers

A darkened room with lit screens

The continual buzz of voices

Jumping from one plane to another

Giving them directions to keep them safe

Rapid, never ending, hum of voices

The supervisor watching the screens ready to "plug in" if needed

Room sized screen showing planes the size of bugs

By the thousands converging across the country as the sun rises and traffic moves

No hesitation, moving magically addressing unseen crews on the other end

Guiding them to their destination

And then one plane ducks and disappears from the screen

A second follows its path

And a third

And across the country, a fourth

Seizing the hearts of all who are watching

Television screens light up, the central command center silent

Then the order comes "Bring them down"

Shut the borders

Land the planes

Any who don't respond will be fighter escorted

The voices increase as the bugs like specs start to disappear

Landing at uncharted destinations

One after the other after the other

Till the room becomes silent

Only military bugs are on the screen

The National Airspace is empty

The saviors of the day sit silent

Then begin to understand the depth of the unfathomable play they starred in

These fearless controllers of the sky

Hiding their faces or embracing each other

And as one soul

They cried.

Opening Pandora's Box

Afraid

Why are the people so Afraid?

Not just our politicians—they use fear as their fuel urging them to do things they don't believe in

Afraid they will be censored or even worse lose their lifetime jobs and benefits

The trickle down of fear stagnates all processes—freezing beneficial reform into political expediency

Not just employers who don't support excellence to pinch the penny for results

Cutting corners, modifying results to achieve quantity not quality

Not just doctors who so fear litigation that they sacrifice the essence of patient responsibility

Mill reaction, waiting rooms of waiting patients, stamp diagnosis and treatment

Not just investment counselors who prefer limos to good advice

Not just landlords who ignore issues of tenants till they quit complaining

"I don't respond till they complain three months on one issue, then I raise their rates"

When did our beliefs turn to fear—afraid to do our jobs correctly, afraid to speak out, afraid to vote our conscious—Afraid

The victims of the "AFRAIDS" are not just the poor—they are not Native American, African American, Hispanic, Basque, Italian, Portuguese, Arab, Jewish, Christian, Latino, Immigrant, Citizen, neighbor, cousin, brother, self

They are us—falling into the same divide—Afraid.

"Isms"

Our world is suffering from the disease

Keeps spreading, relentless killer of self

Isms running amok through the streets and alleys

No seeming way to stop the spread

Wrong color—racism

Wrong gender—sexism

Pros and Cons screaming in the streets

Waving their signs that only the cameras read—activism

Men deciding a woman's right to choose

Straights deciding if gays should marry

White supremacist defining liberty

Recloak the Statue of Values, paint her white, wrap her in jewels

I am the center of the universe—egotism

I will only vote the way my party wants because I am afraid not to—politicism

I am rich and you are poor and that will never change—capitalism

You will do as I say or disappear—communism

Only one religion, Hinduism, Buddhism, Catholicism, Mormonism—too many isms to count

Fills our brains, fills our hearts

Fills our news, fills our ear canals

Makes our minds blur then slowly shut down

No reason to think because we can't escape or change or modify

So, we blindly accept that we can't impact

The isms.

Earth Day

Benevolent, so filled with self-applause

We honor our home, our mother earth

The most magnificent, most omnipotent

We give the world ONE day of recognition

While we hid away from the deadly plague

Letting nature be in charge

Our waterways no longer clogged

With oil-spewing ships and litter-tossing thoughtlessness

Exhaust-belching cars' engines turned off

Trees sighing a breath of relief

Orcas breaching in unexplored harbors

Free to fly without fear

Birds riding the updrafts

Urban corridors their new runway

As they celebrate in songs that resounded off the concrete

As humans reopen their doors

As we return to our hurly-burly lives

So self-important, so in charge

Will we remember what it felt like

When the earth got more than one day.

Nag

The laptop says "tell me what you want to do."
I don't know how to answer.
It's only 10:30 and I am lost.
My mind has been sending bad signals—
Resentments that don't even matter.
Silly scrapes and ego scratches
That don't even matter.
But they nag.
Neighbor, girlfriend, co-worker, pushy
Nagging at the back of my brain.
Surely, I have more to do in my life.
Surely, I have more to add.
Nag, nag, nag,
Nobody home, nag.
"Tell me what you want to do."
Not a clue.
Nag.

Not in a Good Place to Write

I said to myself, "I'm not in a good place to write."

Chasing internal dragons in my head

Hiding from ghosts self-made

Tools needed, not weapons, a late-night talk with a new comrade

A message from a friend who will always be there for me

The cat saying, "I need you" as she looks up into my eyes

What better place to write?

Caring outside my space, bringing others in

Opening the blinds covering my eyes

Opening myself to sounds beyond my cries

As the spirit moves from self to others

It takes me with it

Showing me that life is still there

Calming my mind and renewing its presence in me

I'm in a good place to write

Lead my fingers across the keys

Writing a message to—

Me.

Not Giving Up

Who am I to give up?
Quitting the battle
Removing the armor of life
Who am I to dig a hole
And pull the covers over my head?
Taking my toys and going home
Because it's not going my way
But wait—this IS home
The world's floors need swept
The laundry done
Little critters need petted
Giving, filling my internal void
My face relaxes into a smile
Outside myself and back into the flow
Grabbing with both hands
The beauty of the Spirit
Getting UP
Not giving up

Transition

That space in time between
What is and what might be
The seasons teach us through demonstration
Their color foliage to empty leaves
To new growth and bright birth hues
Our youth teach us through waddles to walks
To running feet throughout the house
Transition.
Our calendars mark the days
With celebrations of transition
Holidays of thanks and giving, of new beginnings
Transition.
Mirroring the model of life
We transition as well
Stage by stage as we watch
The Rubix's cube of our lives
Align the colors to celebrate victory
A life well spent
A life well shared
A celebration of
Transition.

Need

I need more butterflies and volunteer flowers
I need more cotton candy sunsets and gentle breezes
I need more feelings of love and acceptance
I need, I need,
I need to send more butterfly presents
I need to send more celebrations of volunteer flowers
I need to pay attention to the gentle breezes
I need to share more feelings of love and acceptance
I need to see the need in the eyes of my brothers
Is need, in fact, the Spirit in me opening my eyes?

Turning off the News

Contrails draw abstract art in the sky as the upper air distorts their perfect lines and turns them into a painting unsurpassed by mere viewers below.

Birds rule in the cacophony of choruses emanating from the wild area—that stretch of real life that separates the preposterous designs of humans with the unparalleled work of nature's architect.

Bare feet in sand and pebbles, green grass performing as buffers and eye candy for the observer: perfect hiding place for ants and little wanderers traversing occupied territory.

Disrupter is my role, not chosen but a part of my nature, like the coyote that has been sneaking a peak at my cat in the middle of the night.

Checking out the fortifications to see if screen and cat door and motion lights can really defend from perpetrator or if that furry appetizer is worth the effort.

Not last night, thank you for moving on.

Two bunnies playing romp entertain me over my morning coffee—better than the news.

Amazing how long those roles have lasted and perpetuate; amazing how fragile our view and how short sighted is ours.

Saber rattling to build self-edifying egos.

Gold Gods to self—written in taunts and screams and shouted epitaphs to—

The bunnies are back—playing leap frog like we did as kids; laughing in the grass as they run in search of another nibble from the flower bed.

Cat is snoozing wrapped in her self-designed coil of fur and paws—making little snore sounds and paw spasms as she chases the rabbits and birds in her dreams.

I observe.

I observe.

I breath and turn off the news.

I return instead to the essence of life.

The true message, the voice of God that resonates in my body, in the cat, in the rabbits, in the birds—even in the coyote.

I observe and I whisper "Thank you, God."

COVID

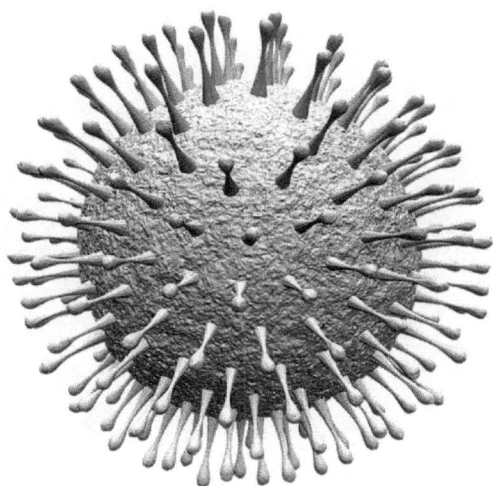

Smiling with a Mask

The mask is making my nose run

It tickles as I walk down the grocery store aisle

Don't sneeze, don't sneeze, please don't sneeze as I pass a woman with a baby in her cart

I smile at her little one, lift my eyes and smile at her

She smiles back

I can tell because her eyes light up

Kindness can't be hidden, caring fills the space around me

Opening the blinds that cover my eyes

Opening myself to sounds beyond my cries

The Lord takes me on its journey

Showing me life is still there

An extra can of soup lightens the grocery sack

Handing it to the man on the curb, there go those eyes again

Sharing a late-night talk with a new comrade in the journey

A friend sending me teddy bear love mimes to make me laugh

As the spirit moves me from self to others

So many reasons to smile

My Mother's voice in my head reminding me

To DO UNTO OTHERS, I first must remember—they are there.

Grief

Grief, a single word whose width and depth equates to an aphorism

The finest thoughts in the fewest words

Hearing the word paints vivid pictures

To every ear that hears, every mouth that quivers as pictorials of the word

Fill every heart with memories

Dealing with loss is like peeling the petals of a rose

Each layer blesses us with a gift

Its beauty, its scent, its softness and yes

The pain of its thorns

The memories of the blessing of life

The mental faces that will never fade—will never age

But will live in our hearts forever

The true definition of immortality

Grief is the healer that frees

Our spirit to take wing

And like the rose, bloom again.

Wondering Aloud

Wondering aloud—on paper—who we are.

Not just the "we" of my friends and family but the world "we"

Probably the first time—really, since the Ark.

Maybe a stretch but our WWI and II touched but did not touch everywhere—everywhere

People say, "this is not greater than the influenza," and I have to think—seriously WORLDWIDE

I think it is hard for us to grasp more than the numbers, which are catastrophic, but the breadth

Real Worldwide—all within a few months—Real worldwide

I think about what that means.

The true aborigines, so safe from the mental contamination of the outside world, now contaminated by "us" anyway?

The sacred providers of learning and healing worldwide that bring with them the teaching of the past

Whole aborigine and Native American villages of knowledge and guidance being decimated and with them the keys to understanding from a viewpoint not yet absorbed and understood in the world ecosystem

Our world is losing people but with it we are losing pieces of our Museum of Knowledge

It is being replaced by people rushing to the streets to bear arms, wear red hats, demand a freedom from isolation

It is being replaced by street parties and packed restaurants—FREE AT LAST—THANK GOD ALMIGHTY WE ARE FREE AT LAST—defined in an entirely different way

Defined now by people who have always been blessed and always allowed to be self-focused

Defined now by people who don't care about anyone or anything except for the center of their universe—themselves

So now the big question becomes: Will our lives just go back to where they were? If, and only if, they dramatically change over the long-haul, will that mean that they come back to self-centered life-styles? Does that mean pre-C-19 standards, where we all pretend to give a damn about our fellow man as long as it doesn't impede my life, will again be our standard?

Interesting thoughts we can have

But will we?

Centering

Limitless Life

Migrating starlings form waves of wings across the sky

Moving as one

Raising and soaring, diving and floating

A cacophony of of wings cutting through the air

Many beating to the same drummer

Free and limitless yet joined by invisible strings

Holding together a band of gravity warriors

Cutting their trail across the sky

Their energy seeping into every pore of the observer

The spirit blessing us with a reminder

Of limitless life.

Peace

Peace—interesting word

Doesn't need defined or described—just felt

Starts at my toes when the sun pokes in

Stretches to my "little one" lying on my belly

No definition needed—she loves me

Spreads to my consciousness to clean the cobwebs—even the corners

Flows to my limbs to test their strength

Challenge them for another day

Peace

Shared by my yard's view; incorporates the tree the squirrels and birds share with me

Watching the dancing game of cat and squirrel and birds and rabbits

Always aware of each other but always in their own protected world of

Peace

The calm enters the depth of my being as I celebrate life

Forgetting the trials

Forgetting the pain

Remembering Peace

Remembering the amazing Spirit who brought me the gift

Winking at Michael's picture as I head to the bathroom

To start another day

Another day fostered by a little spark

Called Peace

Thank you, God.

Our Universe

We are a dust spec on the screen of the limitless universe

If you focus closer you will see galaxies formed by planets

Planets to continents

Continents to countries to states to counties to cities to—

To you

To me

To us

As we lift the magnifying glass to include our family, our friends, our church, our outreach

No longer minuscule me but limitless me

Brothers and sisters joining arm in arm

No matter what our divergent beliefs or biases

Joining arm in arm

Forming our city

Our county

Our State

Our country

Our continent

Our planet

Our galaxy

Our amazing dust spec in the limitless universe.

lights

Bright lights and glowing wreaths

Ornate celebration of life

Sending our greetings to the world beyond us

We celebrate with lights—man's attempt to share joy

Fireworks, neon temptress urging you inside

Houses decked with twinkling color

Sometimes celebration, sometimes to compete?

We sometimes forget we are surrounded by

A different celebration of light

Lightning turning the night sky into day

The cotton candy performance of sunrise and sunset

A magical light-show with which ours cannot compare

The jewels of life around us every day

God's light in our eyes as we celebrate love

Give love, feel love, sharing the magic

God's greatest gift to mankind

The ability to love.

The Sun Still Shines

Good Friday and Easter

Days on the calendar that mark transition

Transition from winter's hibernation to spring's blossoming

Days that represent a carpenter from nowhere

Whose impact is still felt world-wide over 2000 years later

Sandals and the robe of the poor

Whose voice still resonates in our world of mass media and social networking

A carpenter rises still above all our chatter

Entered a city as a hero, was turned on by the same throngs

Carried the cross that he was sacrificed on

That all these thousands of years later is the hallmark of eternal life

A voice that still resonates

Reminding us of our blessings as we carry our own crosses

Our own challenges

Our eyes open to see our brothers

Carrying their own crosses—all the same weight

And if they stumble, we reach out a hand to help them regain their balance

And we walk on together

Celebrating the majesty of life

As the bird's song celebrates the majesty of spring.

Fresh Start of Hope

A Fresh Start

Have you ever wanted to call a timeout and request a "do over"?

Requested a fresh start, forget yesterday, and erase that word you said or that act you performed

Put behind you what is past and plow ahead

Ignoring rear view mirror—full steam ahead

A fresh start

But wait—isn't every second fresh

The people we love never left each other

We were continually joined in love, in common respect

Bound together in something neither time nor distance can unbind

United in a mutual search for and understanding of

The true meaning of life

Recognition of the Spirit that binds us together

The Spirit that warms our hearts when we think of each other, quirks, and all

Every second is a fresh start for us all

Perhaps not now in person but always joined in spirit

Thank you all for sharing this fresh start with me

A new second of enlightenment, a new second of understanding

A new second of celebration

A fresh start because I blinked my eyes, because I took a breath

Every second, a fresh start.

Normal

Normal

The eye of the beholder Offers a Murky view

Eyes glazed over with lenses colored by past

Colored by uneasy definition of future

Normal

Definition once so easy—not so much anymore

Shifting axis of our world—redefinition of the universe

Normal?

Nothing in the mirror reflects what was once there

Something else reflects back at me

Unsettling, unsure, no swagger—shyness peeking around a corner at me

Hiding its face in a mask of uncertainty

Normal visits the recesses of my mind

Peeking out but not showing itself—not yet

Waiting to be defined, redefined

Shy little glimpses—come out and play with me again

Normal

An Instrument

Instrument—a tool for delicate work

Reassembling broken pieces of the fine china of life

Delicate work

Hearts streaming tears down stressed faces

Dark shadows protecting the corridors of fear

Reaching for a spark of light

A reason to succeed

A reason for hope

Delicate work

Mending torn curtains, mending fences

Becoming an instrument necessitates exposure

Exposing the instrument to vulnerability

Delicate work

Calling on the strength outside and inside

Help me be a tool for delicate work.

God's Library

God's library has trillions of books

You don't need a library card or Amazon account

Just taking a moment to observe

Opens pages of amazing knowledge

Insights unimaginable

Books inside the eyes of the people you meet

The furry friends that share their life with you

The miracles of the world around you

Some books easily open their pages

When they see you wanting to read

Others with lowered lids protect their pages

Still others only show their cover

Even while they innocently announce how open they are

But hide their truth in bright eyes and welcoming smiles

A simple tree whose bark hides the layers within

Till a branch leaves its trunk

And shows us the miracle that they are

An open book

Part of the endless library

Everywhere we look if we choose to read

The library is open

Come read with me.

The Hawk

A hawk flew into my tree today, unannounced

Not like the woodpeckers who knock on my gutters before migrating to my tree

Asking permission by driving me crazy with their beaks on metal

Permission granted

No, this guy just moved in

Eyeing my cat through the screen, my visiting rabbits suddenly missing their afternoon tromp

Uninvited

He took a couple of graceful dives and snatched what seemed to be a bug

Mission accomplished then back to my tree

Suddenly, as I was watching his uninvited antics, his eyes focused on me

We watched each other, staring into each other's eyes

It was calming, gentle, quiet, peaceful even

Then I realized, it was not my tree but his.

Healing

My oak tree bears the scars of trimming

Removing branches to save the roof that protects me from
the elements

Scaring the noble oak whose newly hewn flat eyes watch me

Preceded by other amputations that have now formed
interesting faces

Spelling the history of the great oak

I watch now as new branches appear

New leaves sprout

Squirrels have found new routes

To bypass the missing and utilize the old, feed off the new

The scars heal with twigs of green

Or form faces in the bark which announce to the world

"I am stronger than the loss

I am stronger than the saws

Watch me heal

Learn from me

Watch me heal"

And the birds test the strength of the new

And pronounce it strong enough to hold their nest

Strong enough to support tomorrow.

You Are Not Broken

You are not broken—maybe bending?

Willows laugh at us in the wind

As we fight to right ourselves

They bend and smile

It is their given to make those amazing sounds

Their song is their contribution

To the melody played by the wind

Feel it in your hair, feel it against your skin, feel it in your soul

You are not broken, enjoy the bending

As the spirit teaches you the song of the willows.

Disappointment/Opportunity

Disappointment/Opportunity both such intriguing words

Book definitions of each lack

Until, that is, you internalize

Merge each with your core

Words are just words without the Spirit

They only exist when integrated in the essence of your very being

Wrapped in the package of self

Its ribbon's tensile strength bolstered by the hand of God

As eyes are opened and vision clears

We discover the truth

Disappointment/Opportunity

They are the same

When we shake off the pain and walk.

Clouds

Clouds—such amazing transmittal mechanisms

Storytellers

Puffy white shapes that remind us of characters

Or platforms to develop our own stories

No one else gets to judge our interpretation

Of the gift that the Spirit sends us each day

In our magical gift of–clouds

Spirit revealing to us through puffs of foam

Or thunderous expressions

The message we need to deeply clutch to our chest

Through the lightning and thunder

Through the burning sun

The message remains the same

Love

Uncompromising, irrepressible, undefinable love

Revealed—in the blessing of Clouds.

Searching for an Ending

So, what do I do now?

I checked my emails

Had my two conference calls

So, what do I do now?

I have no hobbies—none intrigue me

I can't walk the beach or the neighborhood

What do I do now?

What is my life ahead of me?

And is it a trail I really want to experience?

I can barely walk

What is my future?

I always so looked forward

Now I look back

Is that the definition of aging?

Looking in the rearview mirror with smiles

Looking forward with trepidation

Alone again

Like the loneliness I felt as a searcher for love

Now a searcher for an end

What do I do now?

The Blessing of a Day

The magic marker sky

Peeked through my window this morning

My cat stretched on my lap

And gave me the look of expectation—feed me

Testing my limbs to see if it was safe to stand

I started my day

That few minutes gave me courage

Gave me resolve

Gave me thankfulness and strength

Till the magic marker sky

Kisses me Good Night

And my purring cat returns to my lap

And once more, I am blessed with a day.